DARK TRUTHS

HERU THE FIRST SON

DARK TRUTHS

Jason Thomas

CONTENTS

Dedication
vii

1 — Introduction
1

2 — The Light vs. the Dark
4

3 — Freedom vs. Security
11

4 — Conspiracy Theory
15

5 — Fear Factor
24

6 — Criminal Justice
30

7 — What is Wrong With Black Americans?
36

8 — The Machine Consciousness
47

CONTENTS

9 — Money Matters (Or Does It?)
56

10 — We Now Return to Your Regularly Scheduled Programming
68

About The Author
73

To Jason, Jahara, Jace and Jaiel; your father's small contribution to a better world for you all,

Copyright © 2020 by Heru the First Son

All rights reserved. No part of this book may be reproduced in any manner whatsoever without written permission except in the case of brief quotations embodied in critical articles and reviews.

First Printing, 2020

INTRODUCTION

Do you want to know the truth? Before you read this manuscript, you should ask yourself this question. Most people believe that they want to know the truth but I find that most people are wrong. People that truly want to know the truth about something usually already do. They may not be able to prove it or to explain why the truth is what it is. They may not even be able to put what they know into words, but they know it nonetheless. This is because the truth is not rocket science. It is not difficult to see; it simply is what it is. In fact, it is more difficult to hide the truth than it is to see it.

On the other hand, a person who does not know the truth about something usually doesn't want to. This is because, when the truth about something is ugly and not what a person wants to hear, they will reject the truth and refuse to accept it and there is no amount of convincing or proving that can be done to make that person accept what is obviously the truth. A person who is in denial of the truth will cling to every false explanation or rationale and every exception to the rule that they can to back their denial. But it still doesn't change the truth from what it is to what they want it to be.

What you will find in this manuscript is the truth, pure and simple. What you will not find is a bibliography or footnotes. I will not cite my sources to you or go out of my way to prove to you that what I'm saying is true. There are two reason for this. The first reason I have already stated in the first two paragraphs of this introduction. The second reason is that some of the most deceitful people writing some of the most deceitful material known to man have tried to masquerade that material as truth using footnotes and citing sources. All the while, they are manipulating the information, taking bits and pieces of the work of others and spinning the meaning to suit their purposes.

So, the reading of this manuscript will be an exercise in the use of intuition on the part of the reader. As the reader, you will be required to use your own intuition to assess the truth of what is written here for yourself. If you truly wish to know the truth about a subject that is covered in this manuscript, then through the use of intuition, you will find it here. On the other hand, if you are a person who finds it difficult to accept unpleasant truths, then Krishna, Buddha, Muhammad, Jesus Christ or the Almighty Himself could be cited in the footnotes as a source and you still wouldn't recognize the truth, so that is pointless.

Ultimately, there is no motive or goal in the writing of this manuscript other than for the truth to be spoken, in plain English. Those who have ears to hear and eyes to see, let them do so now.

THE LIGHT VS. THE DARK

I would like to begin this manuscript by going over a basic principle that I believe will help the truly gifted and open-minded reader mentally. In our culture the words "light" and "dark" have opposite and very heavy connotations. We see the light as good and pleasant. In the light, we feel that there is little to fear, that everything is illuminated and easy to see, and things in general are bright, colorful and pleasing to the eye. On the other hand, we tend to see the dark as bad and unpleasant. In the dark, we feel that there is much to fear, that everything is hidden and difficult to see, and that things in general are threatening, and inscrutable to the eye. The idea of the dark is very uncomfortable to a people who depend on sight as their primary way of analyzing the world around them.

Now that we have dealt with the popular ideas about the light and the dark, let us go beneath the surface to understand the truth about them. The fact of the matter is that light gives rise to a whole host of illusions and effects that deceive the mind. In the dark there is no illusion. To explore this assertion, let us start with the science of color. In reality color is created when light strikes an object and that object absorbs all wavelengths of light except one or so. We'll just say one for the sake of simplicity. The one wavelength that is not absorbed is reflected back to the eye, and the brain interprets the color of the object as red or blue or whatever wavelength of light that was not absorbed. If this is the scientific explanation of how color is produced, then if you really think about it, color is nothing more than an optical illusion. The color of an object is not an inherit trait of the object itself. An object has no color without light. An orange is not orange unless light strikes it.

Another illusion produced by light that deserves examination is reflection. When you look into a mirror you see yourself and the world around you looking back at you. The scientific explanation of how a reflection is produced is that light strikes a surface that is so smooth that the light is reflected directly back to the source. Is there really and identical you, living in a world looking exactly like your own, looking back at you, existing in that mirror? No. When you eliminate the light, will you see a reflection in that mirror? No. Once again, reflection is not an inherent quality of a mirror. Without light, a mirror is simply a very smooth surface.

Many people and children are afraid of what they call

the dark but what ends up being, in reality, low levels of light. They are afraid under these conditions primarily because they can't see well, but also, because the shadows in these conditions are more ominous and deceiving. The irony of this, of course, is that the darkness is not responsible for the shadows, rather it is that bit of light that remains that is responsible for the ominous and deceiving shadows. In total darkness, shadows do not exist.

Now if we take a moment to examine the attributes of darkness, we will find an interesting difference from light. Although it is true that darkness robs a person of their sight, it is also true that there is very little illusion in the dark. When you touch an object, the texture of that object is what it is. It will remain the same when the light is turned on. Likewise, with taste and smell. And if you hear something in the dark, rest assured something moved to produce that sound. I'm sure that those of you who know a blind person who has learned to compensate for his/her lack of sight with his/her other senses can attest to the fact that it is far more difficult to deceive that person than one might think.

Now my motive in all of this comparison is not to villainize light. It is an attempt to encourage an objective state of mind in the Westerner (my original target audience) who has some very deeply rooted attitudes toward the concepts of light and dark. The comparisons also form the framework for a metaphor that will lead us to deeper truths about society in general throughout this manuscript.

The metaphor, as it applies to the subjects covered in this manuscript, basically will take this form: The light, as it applies to people and society in general, corresponds to that which people will tell you about what motivates them and why they do what they do. The light corresponds to the news and constitution and the things we as citizens want to believe about our nation and what drives it and rules it. The light is what people will say and believe because it sounds good and right. The dark corresponds to that which people won't tell you about what really motivates them and why they do what they do. The dark corresponds to what really goes on under the cover-ups, the spins created by the media, and violations against the people by covert-ops organizations, corporations, and false "justice" establishments and organizations. The dark is what people won't say and/or believe because it seems bad and wrong.

As in the earlier comparison, the light is full of illusions. The light is full of aesthetically pleasing things that we as humans want to believe are true but, in fact, may not be. On the other hand, in the dark there exist nothing but the truth. You will find a lot of ugly things in the dark such as bigotry, greed, racism, sexism, etc., but no matter what you find in the dark, it will be the truth.

What you find in the dark is what truly motivates a person, organization, or event. Take a Corvette, Cadillac or Mustang for example. They are beautiful cars on the outside. The shape of the car, the paint job, the glossy finish. But none of the things that make the car beautiful make it move and serve its basic purpose. The, engine, which by most accounts is decidedly less beautiful than the outside of the car, is what makes the car move, and once you close the hood what is the engine shrouded in? Darkness.

Now I'm not saying here that a person, an organization or an event cannot have honorable and aesthetically pleasing reasons and motivations. The thing about that, however is that if a person or organization has honorable motivations and aims, chances are those motivation and aims have been broadcast ad nauseum thus, those motivations and aims have not remained in the dark, have they? In addition to that, you can bet your bottom dollar that those people and institutions are tempered by practical concerns such as the finance required to self-sustain, the politics around what is being dealt with, self-preservation, etc.

What I am saying is that if there are less than honorable motivations moving a person, an organization (especially organizations), or an event, nine times out of ten those motivations will stay in the dark. It is up to us as discerning seekers of truth to go beneath the surface and brave the darkness to find the truth of something. This idea takes on critical importance when applied to ourselves as citizens of a country that claims to be governed "by the people, for the people."

DARK TRUTHS

Most people don't want to deal with life's ugly truths. Most Americans don't want to entertain the idea that their government might be involved in less than honorable activities at home and abroad or that their government may even conspire against its own citizens at times. They don't want to entertain these notions because it shakes their sense of safety and security. It makes them uneasy and leaves them feeling exposed. However uncomfortable it may be, it is nonetheless imperative that those who would govern themselves and control their own destinies deal with life's ugly truths and brave the darkness. Why? Well, if you have not been able to infer this from the forgoing, I will put it plainly: in the darkness is where the power lies.

Now at this point in the manuscript, I believe it is time for me to lay down a couple of disclaimers so that readers will be better able to understand where I'm coming from. My first disclaimer is that I am not aligned with any particular organized religion. I have studied much material from many religions. Enough to know that if mankind spent half as much time concentrating on what we agreed on rather than our differences, we would have long ago entered a golden age and known the face of the Most High. But religion is not my concern right now. My only allegiance is to truth. My second disclaimer is that I am not writing this manuscript from a particularly ethnocentric standpoint. It is true that I happen to be an African American man and I am real enough to admit that I would like to see my people doing better, involving themselves in nation building and increasing their power and independence but, I am at a point in my life where I have come to terms with things as they are in the world, not as I would like them to be. My last and perhaps most important disclaimer to understanding this manuscript is that I am not making any moral judgements in this manuscript. I may reveal some rather unsavory truths about people, organizations, or events within the following pages but at no point am I personally assigning a value to what is. For example, I may say that a person or institution is motivated by racism. Conventional wisdom would interpret that I am saying that it is bad that they are motivated by racism. I am not. I'm simply saying that racism motivates them. Period. In the light, people always try to assign a value to everything. In the darkness, things simply are what they are.

Now that I have laid down the basics for better understanding of this manuscript, I believe we can safely proceed. If you as the reader have been able to intuit, discern and understand any truth at all from that which has been written thus far, then I strongly believe that you will glean much food for thought from the following pages. Enjoy.

FREEDOM VS. SECURITY

We as Americans value our freedom greatly. We value our ability to pursue whatever sane goals that we choose to pursue; and even a good amount of not so sane goals. We value our ability to get up and go where we wish when it suits us. We like to be able to do pretty much what we want as long as our actions don't encroach upon the freedoms of others. We also greatly value our right to privacy.

As Americans, we also value the sense of security that we get from knowing that we live in a military super power. American citizens wrap ourselves in a comfortable feeling of superiority to the rest of the world based on the military power and economic dominance of our nation. We also have a pretty good sense of internal security as well, especially those of us in the right neighborhoods. In America, the privileged, the middle class, and even, to some extent, the lower middle class can take comfort in the fact that American law enforcement bodies will minimize their chances of being victimized by crime. All that has been written in this chapter thus far can be considered ideas and notions that exist in the light, and not altogether untrue.

The truth about freedom and security that exists under the surface in a slightly darker realm however, is that freedom and security enjoy a certain relationship. That relationship is polar opposite. What images come to mind when you think about freedom? For me, I imagine open spaces, blue skies, and nothing hindering me from doing what I wish to do or going where I want to at any given moment. When you think of security, what images come to mind? For me, it brings to mind images of walls, gates, guards, etc. Now of course, we would intend and prefer for such fortifications to keep threats out as opposed to keeping us in but in reality, wherever you put a wall or a gate, it keeps things in just as much as it keeps things out.

My point in all of this is to bring to mind the realization that there is a tradeoff and a situation of balance at work here. In order to have more freedom, one has to give up some security and vice versa. With the tragic events of 9/11, Americans got to see firsthand the opposing relationship of freedom and security. At first, the shock and fear created by the events caused the American public to clamor for action to be taken to ensure the safety and security of the nation and bring the terrorists to justice. Then, as the initial shock and fear caused by 9/11 wore off and the Bush Administration continued to steadily encroach on American civil liberties in the name of "national security," the American public began to second guess the wisdom of relinquishing freedom in the name of security.

Now, I know that I promised earlier that I would avoid making value judgements but, at this point I feel compelled to add my two cents. I promise, though, that anytime that I do this throughout this manuscript, I will be upfront about the fact that I'm making a value judgement, implied or otherwise. At any rate, in my humble opinion, security could never trump freedom. I have been a prisoner before and, contrary to popular belief, prisoners are some of the most secure people on earth. Yes, there can be problems and threats within the prison community, but for those who are not problem-oriented or into creating problems for themselves, prison life is mind-numbingly secure; in other words, boring. You know exactly what to expect from day to day. There is no need to wonder what's going to happen tomorrow. A prisoner can rest soundly knowing that it is highly unlikely that any threat originating from outside the prison walls will be allowed in to harm him. You see, most people fail to understand that part of the beauty of freedom is uncertainty. Part of the beauty is not knowing what tomorrow might bring, or what you might get into the next day.

Now, I admit that there are certain things in life that we as humans would prefer to be secure, such as food, clothing and shelter. When we explore deeper in the darkness, however, we find a shocking irony. The irony is that both freedom and security are simply illusions; security probably more so than freedom. I know it may be hard to swallow, but think of nature and the physical world. Absolute freedom is not possible. Absolute security is also not possible, in-fact, I'm not quite sure that security exists at all. A tragedy of the highest order could befall a man in the comfort and security of his own home. Whether a man becomes paralyzed in a gun battle in the middle of the street, or paralyzed from a nasty spill down his stairs, it doesn't change the fact that he is paralyzed. Life is funny like that.

Ultimately, for us as humans, and moreover as American citizens, to believe that we can be totally free or totally secure is absurd at best, and for us to believe that we can actually be both at the same time is completely ludicrous. So, what do we do with this revelation? Well, therein lies the reason for the importance of a people who aspire to govern themselves to brave the darkness and deal with the difficult questions and sticky issues found there. Our power lies in our freedom to choose how we want to live. Knowing the truth about things is the only way to make well-informed decisions. Well-informed decisions have a better chance of being wise decisions. As I stated earlier, in the darkness is where the power lies.

CHAPTER 4

CONSPIRACY THEORY

It is said that what is done in the dark must eventually come to light. When people are actively seeking the truth and are willing to accept the truth for what it is when confronted with it, this statement holds true. On the other hand, when people are not actively seeking the truth and are not willing to accept it, then what's done in the dark tends to stay there.

During the last decades of the 20th century, there had been a moderate groundswell of public interest in what is generally referred to as conspiracy theory; especially toward the onset of the millennium. The interest intensified somewhat after the events of 9/11 as the public tried to make sense of how our government could allow something like that to happen. The media at some point toward the end of the 20th century began a subtle campaign aimed at trivializing conspiracy theory in general. The media started to regularly portray conspiracy theory as paranoid flights of fancy and to characterize the people who went about digging up dark truths as crackpots and whack jobs with questionable sanity. It is a well-known technique. If you want to create doubt in the minds of people as to the accuracy and reliability of certain information and you can't disprove the information; simply discredit the source.

So once again, into the darkness we go to reveal the truth about conspiracy theory, and the truth about conspiracy theory is that it is not theory at all. It is reality, and a rather simple matter really. The moment that the American government began to form covert operations and covert intelligence organizations to reduce the transparency of the government, and the moment the American government began to believe that it was appropriate for them to wage quiet wars in small countries without the knowledge or consent of the American public, that was the precise moment at which the American government began to conspire against the people. Honestly, it's not rocket science and it doesn't require a mountain of evidence to prove, although you can be sure that a mountain of evidence does exist. Many before have done due diligence in exhausting detail on the various conspiracies and scandals that the American government has been involved in through their covert ops and military organizations, but it is not my aim to name and detail them in this manuscript.

My point here is simply that when a government begins to withhold information about its doings and begins to engage in significant operations such as military strikes overseas without the knowledge and consent of the public, it is at that point conspiring against the people. What other secrets are being kept? To better illustrate my point, I'll use the following example. If you were in a marriage and you found that your spouse was keeping a multitude of significant secrets from you, like doing things with your joint finances without your knowledge or consent, would you not begin to wonder what sort of union you were in and what other secrets are being kept from you? It's a common sense reaction, unless of course, you are in denial.

Now, military and intelligence officials will tell the public that they withhold information for security reasons and in some instances that may be true. The truth of the matter however, is that often public approval is not sought and information is withheld because they know that a good portion of the American public, if not the majority, would have a major problem with many of the activities that they are involved in. To them, public opinion is a nuisance that they would prefer not to be bothered with when pursuing their aims. They want to be able to operate with impunity and without public accountability. Now, I'm not sure what you think, but I'm pretty sure that the founders of the American system of government created our system of government the way that they did for the exact purpose of preventing the government from operating without public accountability.

Indeed, the founders of this system of government created the system to run in a transparent manner, and to always ultimately be accountable to the people. The system of checks and balances at the core of the government is meant to limit the power of each branch of government for a reason: power corrupts. So, at the heart of the matter here is, when you think an organization like the C.I.A., that operates not only without the public knowledge of their specific activities, but also without most of the rest of the government's knowledge of their specific activities, where are the checks and balances for their power? Can this sort of unchecked power lead to corruption and even conspiracy against American citizens?

The answer, of course, is yes. In the late 1990's the C.I.A. quietly declassified a file that suggested, or even detailed, C.I.A. involvement in drug distribution; particularly the large-scale introduction of crack cocaine in the black community. Feel free to research this yourself because, at this point, it's a pretty well-known fact. Crack, of course, went on to become a devastating scourge and epidemic in the black community and eventually broke those barriers to become a pretty widely used drug by the white population as well. At one point, statistics showed that there were more white crack users than black, despite media depictions and prison representation. Again, feel free to research that yourself. What's more, they did this as part of an effort to finance one of their quiet wars overseas that the public didn't know much about. I would say that this is a clear-cut example of the CIA abusing their power to act without public knowledge or approval.

In fact, evidence exists that suggests C.I.A. involvement in all sorts of criminal mischief ranging from experimentation in mind control to assassination of prominent public and political officials here and abroad. I chose to shortly outline their involvement in the crack epidemic for two specific reasons. The first reason is that I am most intimately acquainted with that particular debacle, and, at this point it is probably one of the least debatable. The second reason though, is that the story of the crack epidemic appears to shed light on two often denied or disregarded racial realities in American society. The first is, despite all claims to the contrary, there still exists an extremely venomous form of racism in the power structure of America. The second reality is that there is a less active form of racism that exists in what I can safely say is the majority of Americans that is just as deadly but also ends up backfiring on them in the long run. This form of racism is the kind that allows a reality like the C.I.A. propagation of the crack epidemic in the black community to come to light and for there not to be a huge public outcry from Americans of all colors in response to it.

Now, I'll be the first to admit that the blame for the lack of public outcry falls primarily and squarely on the black community's shoulders for not having enough love for ourselves and concern for the damage that crack did to the community to make a hell of a lot more noise about it than we did (I'll get to that dynamic later on in this manuscript). Aside from that though, white American citizens and indeed American citizens in general have this tendency to witness things that their government does to people overseas and to other races within the U.S. population, and turn a blind eye to it. The basic attitude in this is "as long as the government doesn't do that to me, it doesn't matter" or the fatalistic "you can't beat City Hall." When dealing with a government that has power over you though, this attitude is ultimately self-defeating because eventually, as they say, "the chickens always come home to roost." It's like keeping a vicious dog in your home, and every time you take the dog for a walk, it attacks a stranger without provocation. If you take the attitude that the dog is fine as long as he doesn't attack you and continue to keep the dog in your home without addressing the problem, it is only a matter of time before this dog attacks you or someone else you love. How this concept takes form in regard to the crack epidemic is illustrated by the spillover of crack usage into the white community then, and possibly by the rise of the opioid epidemic ravaging the white community now (I do not believe that it is coincidental that every time the U.S. government occupies a country overseas with poppy fields, an opioid epidemic of some sort ensues in this country). The fact of the matter is that the entire American population should have been up in arm about the fact that the government would dare to basically poison any portion of the US constituency, no matter what color they are.

Another way that you may see the effects of the conspiracy against the American people is through travel. Oftentimes, when Americans who are fortunate enough to travel go overseas and wander out of the glamorized and cleaned up areas designed for tourists, they find themselves in the "real" parts of the country encountering the "real" people of the country. What they find there, in those parts and amongst those people, is a lot of anti-American sentiment and they cannot understand why. What the problem is, most of the time, is that the people of that country know more about what our government has been up to in that part of the world than we do. You see, when the government withholds information about its doings from the people, not only do they rob us of our ability to choose how we want to live, they also rob us of our ability to choose how we want to interact with the rest of the world.

The events of 9/11 were a painful illustration of this truth. Let me begin with a disclaimer that states that I'm personally not sure that everything is what it seems to be as far as 9/11 goes, but I'll address that after dealing with the situation as we have been led to believe it occurred. There is no doubt that the events of 9/11 represent a horrific crime against the American people and there is nothing that could change that fact, but eventually, the logical person arrives at point in his/her thinking where they want to know the motive behind the attack. Knowing your assailant's motives can help you build a profile on your assailant that can be used to better predict your assailant's next move. In other words, knowing what someone's beef is with you will help you better understand how to deal with them.

Now, as a man that is not afraid of the dark, I have no qualms with the idea that one should protect oneself by any means nor do I have any qualms with the idea of eliminating threats to oneself and one's interests. However, as a man of wisdom, I also recognize that, as tempting as vengeance is, it often does nothing more than perpetuate a cycle of violence and contention without end. I also recognize that violence is not the only way to eliminate a threat to oneself. Sometimes, you can eliminate a threat by simply solving the problem between yourself and another party. I'm willing to bet dollars to doughnuts that if we, meaning the American public, were to be somehow enlightened as to what the true nature of the problem is that these "terrorists" have with America, a story involving foul play on the part of our government/military would unfold before us. When our government does dirt overseas without our knowledge or approval, they expose us to retaliation by the wronged and we end up in a situation where we are hopelessly oblivious.

All of this applies only if the events of 9/11 are what they appear to be, of course. I, for one, am not entirely sure such is the case. I have read the work of others who have researched the events of 9/11 in depth, and their research suggests that there may be been elements within our own government that may have allowed or even orchestrated the events of 9/11. What would be the motive behind such a blatant act of betrayal? Well, to accomplish what we have witnessed within the first decade of the millennium, which is the erosion of the rights and freedoms of American society. I know, it seems too diabolical to be true, and many of you may even be considering whether or not I am one of those conspiracy theory guys with questionable sanity mentioned earlier for even suggesting such a scenario. But ask yourself, is what I suggested that far of a step over the line for a government that would perpetuate a drug epidemic in a community of its own citizens, regardless of race?

FEAR FACTOR

There are a variety of tragedies that could befall a person in his/her life. The world is filled with dangers and risks of all sorts. In an earlier chapter of this manuscript, I talked about the opposing relationship that exists between freedom and security. I also expressed my personal opinion that security could never trump freedom for me. Now, there is no way for me to be sure how many readers of this manuscript agree with my view on that, but for those who do, I have a question. What do you think could make a lover of freedom, or anyone for that matter, give up their freedom in exchange for security? If you've guessed that it may have something to do with the title of this chapter, then you are indeed correct. It is fear.

As we all know, fear is a powerful emotion. Fear clouds a person's judgment and can cause people to do and even to believe unwise things. Fear is also an awesome tool that the ruling class has always used throughout history to control the people. In earlier times, the various ruling classes of the world used fear in a direct fashion. By that I mean that rulers sought to have the people fear them. At some point, in the not too distant past I would say, some person, or group of people, was struck with a magnificently clever idea, born of a better understanding of the human psyche. They reasoned that, having the people fear the ruling class directly was probably not the best way to go about controlling them. Using fear directly to control the people tends to breed resentment toward the ruling class in the people. The ruling class must then guard against rebellion from within as well as guard against outside enemies.

The idea that they came up with was to use people's fear indirectly to control them. What that means is, instead of having people fear the ruling class, or in the modern sense, the government, what should be done is to take any and all of people's fears in the world, like invasions from other nations, disease, famine, crime, natural disaster, and anything else you can think of, and whip these fears up within the people to the point where you destroy all sense of self-reliance within the public, and the average person feels like they need a savior, or some kind of help just to face the world every day. You then present the government as that savior, or at least the people's best chance for survival, defense and order in an utterly cruel, chaotic and unforgiving world. The reasoning was that, what you will then see is that people will be more willing to submit to authority with less resentment, even if they don't like much that the governing body is doing, because they feel that the government or ruling class is a necessary evil. Because of the utter fear that you have cultivated in the people for everything, they feel that without the government, their lives would be thrown into utter chaos.

Well lo and behold! The plan turned out to be utter genius and if you've begun to suspect while reading these words that this plan is still being used today on you and I, then once again, you are correct. I challenge you to turn on your evening news program, and I'm willing to bet everything to nothing that the top stories of the evening are mostly, if not all, about crime, terrorism, disaster, tragedy, economic crisis, etc. This is most certainly no coincidence. Some might say that such is simply the nature of the world we live in. I would say that, while it is true that there is much evil in the world, it is also true that if I set out to make record of all the most depraved, disastrous and tumultuous events that I could find in a city, county, country, or the world, I could easily succeed in painting a darker picture of the world than that which may objectively be accurate.

The other explanation you might get for news programs focusing on the stories that they do is that people are entertained by drama, and those are the kinds of stories that get ratings. Funny enough, this is actually true. Despite this truth, there is a critical fact that should be recognized when it comes to the idea of the use of

DARK TRUTHS

fear indirectly to control people. This fact is that the ability to broadcast, through radio and television, was and is absolutely indispensable to the plan to control people through indirect fear. The ability to broadcast allows people with an agenda to place thoughts and fears into the minds of people who may not otherwise have had said thought or fear had they been focused solely on that which is relevant to their lives, in their region, at that moment. Think about the literal meaning of the term "broadcast." To cast something away means to throw it away. Broad means wide and far reaching. It means literally to throw far and wide. In the ancient field of magic, the common saying is a magician casts a spell. Broadcast. Think about that for a while.

At this point, I feel it is necessary to remind my readers that I am not making a value judgment here. My goal is not to villainize broadcasting or even those who use it to their advantage. There are many obvious advantages to broadcasting and there are even some obvious advantages to the idea of controlling people in this fashion, especially when compared to some of the alternative techniques that humankind has seen employed over the ages. My goal is simply to speak the truth. Being consciously aware of the mental games that media plays with us can help us avoid some of the more unpleasant effects that those games can have on us. For instance, whether anyone would like to admit it or not, it is broadcast media that is responsible for a whole host of subtle and not so subtle mental disorders and neuroses that are common to the American public. OCD, hypochondria, anorexia, and bulimia, are but a few of the recognized mental disorders that can largely be caused by the media's constant manipulation of people's fear.

You see, fear is an extremely damaging emotion to the human psyche, especially constant, unwarranted and unnecessary fear. It is my personal opinion that fear is an emotion that man, in his or her spiritual development, should seek to eliminate completely in him or herself. I say this because, based on careful deliberation and my own experience, fear is of absolutely no use and is always crippling. On one hand, fear can cause one to worry oneself into ailment and even death over things that one has absolutely no control over. On the other hand, fear can cause you to take the wrong action or inaction in a situation where you do have some level of control. Either way, it is detrimental.

Ultimately, my goal in this chapter is the same as it has been and will be throughout this entire manuscript. That is, to arm people with the knowledge of the dark; to arm people with the knowledge of intentions that remain unspoken. The why is simple. If you have knowledge of these things, you can better control how they affect you. If, when you turn on your TV, you have conscious knowledge of the intentions of certain elements of your entertainment to affect you in certain ways, you have greater power to enjoy your chosen entertainment without allowing it to affect you in ways you would not choose. Once again, in the darkness is where the power lies.

CHAPTER 6

CRIMINAL JUSTICE

The criminal justice system of this country has been the subject of much debate in the past, and even more so of recent. There is something fundamentally wrong when a country that prides itself on being the land of the free imprisons more of its own citizens than any other country in the entire world, and by no small margin. If we were to take the time to try to decipher what this really means, when we were finished, we would be faced with a set of very disturbing possible implications.

The problem with the criminal justice system is one of those things that exists in our society like the proverbial elephant in the room. Everybody can see that it's there, and everybody knows that it doesn't belong there, but nobody knows just what to do about it, so people just ignore it; at least until it tramples them or someone close to them. In the exploration of this problem, we will find many of the same dynamics at work here that I have touched upon in the earlier chapters of this manuscript.

The criminal justice system exists in the light in the disguise or illusion of justice. A legislative body creates and enacts laws that we are to assume are in the interests of, and are for the greater good of the people who elect the legislators. We then have people, labeled criminals, who break those laws and we are to assume that by doing so, the criminals cause damage to a person or the people as a whole. The idea of justice then calls for the criminal to pay in some way for the damage caused.

When we look at the criminal justice system and the prisons that house criminals that are in the process of paying for their crimes, who we see as the overwhelming racial majorities on the receiving end of this justice are black and Latino men. Neither blacks nor Latinos make up the majority of the American populace. On the other hand, the racial majority of those whom we see on the administering end of this justice, such as judges, lawyers, cops and politicians, is white.

So, what does this ratio imply? Anyone? OK, for those who are shy about this, I'm willing to say it. It implies on the surface that black and Latino men are more prone to criminal behavior for some reason. This, of course, is where we get the justification for stereotyping and racial profiling. Police officers know deep down that this is what they think despite their greatest efforts to avoid stating it outright, and there might even be some truth to it.

OK, so now that I've pulled teeth and said what nobody wants to say because it is not politically correct, it is time to move on to understanding the why of it all. Why are black and Latino men more prone to criminal behavior? Or is the implication nothing more than another illusion? To understand the answers to these questions, we must first understand the black and Latino people and their history. I'll begin by defining who I mean when I say black and Latino.

When I say black people, I mean the descendants of Africans who were kidnapped from their native lands and brought to the Americas to work as slaves. When I say Latinos, I actually mean the people native to the Americas and the surrounding islands. So actually, I mean Native Americans. Native Americans from Mexico, South America, Central America, and certain Caribbean islands acquired the moniker "Latinos" by virtue of Spain being the nation which colonized them, but that doesn't make them any less native to the Americas. Also, new information has recently come to my attention that suggests the possibility that a great majority of who we have come to know as black people are actually Native Americans who were swindled out of their birthright of nativity to this country by means of revisionist history and the first U.S. Census, but that's not yet been confirmed by me personally, and is also a topic for another time. For the sake of brevity, I'll assume that most of my readers have at least a basic knowledge and understanding of the history between the white people of this country and the black and also between the white settlers and the Native Americans. I'll avoid going into exhaustive detail, but for the sake of clarity, I'll touch on it briefly and generally.

We know that the black people of this country came to be here because our ancestors were the victims of the slave trade that helped to enrich Europe and laid part of the foundation for the wealth and power of America today. The Native Americans of the continental U.S. as well as the people native to the Caribbean islands and Puerto Rico were the victims of mass genocide so that their lands could be taken over by Europeans (or at least, that's what we've been told). The people native to Mexico were colonized and enslaved on their own lands for a time and they were also relieved of a good portion of their lands. This is a simplified and concise breakdown of the history of interaction between Europeans and Africans and the indigenous peoples of the lands now called the Americas.

Some may ask what this history has to do with the criminal justice system today. In order to illustrate the connection, we must explore the meaning or purpose of justice. As I stated earlier, criminals are penalized in some fashion in the interests of justice, in order to pay or account for some sort of damage or harm that they caused someone, or the society as a whole. The idea of justice is often represented as a scale. Requiring one to pay for a crime committed against another balances that scale. I now ask, did the Europeans who settled and colonized the Americas not commit innumerable crimes against Africans and Native Americans alike? Was the scale ever truly balanced?

Now whether you believe in spirituality, metaphysics, ancestral/collective memory and the like or not, these things do exist and have a very real and calculable effect on world events and the human mind. For the part of the black and Latino men who seem to have a disproportionate propensity for criminal behavior, they are descendants of people who had crimes of a most horrific nature perpetrated against them without justice, without recompense, without revenge or reparation. Any black or Latino people in the modern day, with any trace of the warrior spirit in them, will find themselves drawn to criminal behavior, at least as it pertains to the mainstream idea of such. That warrior spirit, being as broken and confused as it is in those men at this point, will manifest itself in a variety of ways. The common theme, however, will be resistance or rebellion. The white mainstream, conversely, seeking to maintain the status quo established by the criminal actions of their forefathers, will be completely intolerant of anything even approaching rebellion, specifically from any descendants of the original victims of conquest and enslavement, and will go out of their way to mete out the harshest punishments that they can get away with without destroying the necessary façade of justice.

Crime is crime, despite the European tendency to call their crimes in the New World and Africa "conquering," "conquest" or "colonization." And though the descendants of those colonizing Europeans use the excuse that they should not be responsible for the criminal actions of their forefathers, when a person benefits from ill-gotten gains, does not their very own law normally hold the person who benefits from them accountable, even if said person was not the perpetrator of the crime? Is there not a commonly utilized charge in most jurisdictions called "possession of stolen goods?"

You see, "criminal justice" is a tricky term. A wise man once said that if criminals are tasked with establishing a system of government, a system of legalized crime will be the result. In the light, we are to believe that the term "criminal justice" means justice meted out to criminals who violate the law. The truth that exists in the dark is that the term "criminal justice" actually means justice, the nature of which, is criminal.

CHAPTER 7

WHAT IS WRONG WITH BLACK AMERICANS?

WHAT IS WRONG WITH BLACK AMERICANS?

Some years ago, when I was between 18 and 21 years old, I developed a theory for a condition that I felt was afflicting black Americans today as a result of our collective experiences with white people in America. I called it the Battered Woman Syndrome. Later in life, I heard the same syndrome described in the mainstream. It goes by a different name and it is applied to a different scenario (at least on its face). It is also applied individually as opposed to in the collective manner in which I applied the Battered Woman Syndrome, but I recognize that it is the same syndrome nonetheless. It is called Stockholm Syndrome.

DARK TRUTHS

Stockholm Syndrome refers to a condition that afflicts people psychologically who are caught in a hostage situation for an extended length of time. The captive's fear of his/her captor's wrath will often cause a hostage to focus intensely on pleasing their captor in order to avoid arousing the captor's anger. This is a defense mechanism. If this situation persists for a long enough period of time, the hostage can become so in tune with the preferences and proclivities of his/her captor that he/she begins to identify with his/her captor. This identification can become so strong that the captive becomes allied to the captor more so even than to those who would rescue the hostage, and sometimes captives will even resist rescue.

The Battered Woman Syndrome that I came up with describes the exact same defense mechanism and what happens when the adverse conditions persist long enough for that defense mechanism to solidify in a person's psyche. I simply described it within a different scenario and applied it to black Americans collectively. With the Battered Woman Syndrome, I likened black Americans to a woman who has been violently beaten and kidnapped from her home. Her captor drags her to his home and locks her in his basement. Her captor subsequently proceeds to beat and rape this woman daily. He feeds her the poorest scraps from his tables and forces her to do some manner of hard labor in his basement for his benefit. Over time, as the beatings and rape continue and her hopes of being rescued dwindle, she begins to lessen her resistance, and to give freely of herself to her captor in order to lessen the severity and frequency of the consequences of resistance. She begins to go out of her way to please her captor in order to avoid inciting his wrath upon her. Eventually, she becomes so psychologically damaged that when her captor beats and abuses her, she blames it upon herself, rationalizing that she did something wrong to provoke his abuse.

As time goes on, and her captor is sufficiently satisfied that she is appropriately submissive, he begins to allow her upstairs into his home, confident that she will neither raise a hand against him nor attempt to run away. He begins to feed her a little better than the scraps that she is accustomed to and he allows her to sleep on the carpeted floor of his home. After being so horribly mistreated for so many years, she is so psychologically broken that she is overjoyed at his sudden benevolence, and views it as proof of his true goodness at his core, despite all of the abuse. As a sane person, I ask you; if you were kidnapped, abused and imprisoned without cause or provocation, upon being set free, what would you do? I know that I, once I've resisted the urge to put my foot in the ass of the person who did that to me, would high-tail it back home. She, on the other hand, is so psychologically damaged that she no longer has any desire to go home. Along with the constant abuse, rape, and the fact that she has been living like this for so long that home is a distant memory, let us not forget the fact that for this entire time, her captor has been telling her about the abject poverty and savagery in which she used to live. He tells her that, despite his constant abuse, he has actually improved her situation and rescued her from her horrible living conditions and her own savagery before him. She believes him. All that she thinks she knows about her home is what he tells her, and none of it is good.

So here she is, living in her captor's home now, willingly. Along with the improved treatment that she is receiving from her captor, she also notices and is impressed by the opulence in which her captor lives. She has only the faintest suspicion, if she has any idea at all, that his opulence is a direct result of the hard labor that she was forced to do, as well as a result of what he pillaged from her home during her original kidnapping. It doesn't appear so to her. She doesn't really understand that, after amassing a great deal of wealth thanks to her free labor, he has since been able to invest in new enterprises. Even though it appears to her now that he is rich due to his own ingenuity, she doesn't fully understand that she was the foundation of his current wealth. She now loves and looks up to this man, despite all that he has put her through. He still beats and abuses her periodically, though not with the same frequency, nor level of brutality as in the past. She rationalizes it away as she always has, thinking that she did something wrong to bring the abuse upon herself. This woman is the black American.

That story is a metaphor that outlines the history of

the relationship of black and white people in this country, and also explains the mental condition of black people in America today. There are countless examples of this broken mentality within us and it manifests itself in so many ways. For example, some years ago, a white man named Don Imus made some offensive comments that caused a media stir. He called the women of the Rutgers University women's basketball team "nappy-headed hoes." Initially, he was met with outrage from the black community and, as a result, consternation from his corporate and radio sponsors. This led to his dismissal from his position at his radio station at the time (of course this didn't last long, as he was soon picked up by another).

Suddenly and inexplicably, the focus of the outrage shifted from the white man who felt he could get away with such a comment toward black women, to center on Hip Hop music. I suppose that the rationale of those who led this shift in focus was that Imus learned his terminology and/or disrespect for black women from Hip Hop music. Now, if there is one thing that I know for sure, it is that white men did not learn disrespect for black women (or women in general, for that matter) from Hip Hop. If anything, it's the other way around. As far as the issue of Imus learning his terminology from Hip Hop, it still doesn't justify an attack on our own cultural form of music. Black people need to understand that, just because we use certain terminology amongst ourselves doesn't mean that we owe it to white peo-

DARK TRUTHS

ple to allow them to do the same. We don't. To illustrate this point, I'll use an example of two close friends who may tease each other in certain ways where, if a stranger were to do the same, it would cause a problem. The friends can do that with each other because they are close enough to know that they mean each other no harm. Now, I'm not saying that everything said in Hip Hop is ok, but we should deal with our own issues amongst ourselves privately. When attacked from the outside, our first priority should be to unite and deal with the outsider. What the Don Imus scandal was truly an example of, is the Battered Woman mentality that exists in the black American mind. It is an example of the unwillingness of black Americans to confront, oppose, or hold accountable her captor, who was represented by Imus, and her all too eager willingness to find a way to blame herself for her captor's abuse toward her.

Another, far more serious example of the manifestation of the Battered Woman Syndrome in the black American can be seen in how we view and deal with the problem of crime in our communities. The vast majority of crime in the black community is a direct result of poverty, the despair of oppression, and the Battered Woman Syndrome. These factors are exacerbated by the proliferation of certain hard drugs in our community. As I explained in an earlier chapter, black Americans aren't solely to blame for the crack epidemic. The C.I.A. introduced this drug with what I believe was a long-term strategy in mind. In the 80s, the C.I.A. took what was already a volatile situation, that being poor black communities, and introduced crack which, because of the escapism that poverty inspires and the highly addictive nature of the drug, was a surefire way for black people to make money, although at a devastating social cost to ourselves. Black youth, in their youthful naivete, took to selling the drug in the hopes of escaping the poverty that they had known all their lives. The C.I.A. then made high-powered weaponry available to the black youth, who now had money to afford it and were now vying for control of areas where crack was purchased. The result, of course, was catastrophic. Youth violence and drug addiction, as well as crime in general, skyrocketed in black communities across the nation. This caused the black community to cry out for help from the very same government (her captor) that created the situation in the first place. The government's response was to begin policing black communities with military fervor and to beef up the prison industrial complex, which was very likely all planned from the outset.

I revisit this portion of history because, as a result of it, to this day we have black men languishing in prisons across the nation with ridiculous sentences for selling a drug that they are just as much a victim of as the people who were and are hooked on it. What's really absurd is that even now, after the C.I.A. involvement in the promotion and proliferation of the crack epidemic in black communities has been confirmed, black Americans still allow the American government to characterize, classify and punish our own fathers, brothers and sons as the principle wrongdoers when it comes to crack, or drugs in general for that matter. What's more, those who are more establishment-minded within the black community actually agree with this. Meanwhile, the American government, who in this situation is the original, the largest, and the most malicious perpetrator, is scarcely met with mild consternation, much less any sort of consequence for their actions.

Now, I will admit that altogether, the whole debacle creates a complex issue that is difficult to address or clean up, but the truth of the matter is, once it became public knowledge that the C.I.A. created, or at the very least promoted and encouraged the proliferation of the crack epidemic in black communities, there would have been a much more severe response from black Americans were they not afflicted with this collective case of Stockholm Syndrome that I have been referring to as Battered Woman Syndrome. Black Americans would have collectively mobilized in an aggressive manner and demanded the immediate release of all black men with non-violent crack cases at the very least, and also that the U.S. government pay a very hefty sum for the collective damage to the black communities across the nation. This sort of restoration and remuneration is what happens as a general rule of thumb in any other situation where a people or person is wronged by an organization or individual, yet the idea of reparations for black people is something that people seem to think requires endless debate, including black people themselves. This is yet another crystal-clear example of the Battered Woman Syndrome in the African American mind. We as African Americans simply refuse to hold white people responsible for their actions against us in any substantial or meaningful way, and would much rather docilely accept it and find ways to blame ourselves. The blame is ours ultimately, but not in the manner that most mainstream blacks would like to illustrate it.

I would like to conclude this chapter with a thought that will be difficult for most to understand, but is nonetheless the best way to think about all of this, if not absolutely true. I know that, to those reading this chapter, it may seem as if I am villainizing white people for doing what they have done to black people, and that I believe that they were and are wrong for it. I admit that there was a time when that would be absolutely true, but I have now come to a point in my life where I understand that wrong and right can be extremely relative. I stated in the beginning of this manuscript that in the darkness, things are not right or wrong. They simply are what they are. I hold firm to that assertion.

After our experiences in slavery, black people were acutely aware of how white people viewed us, and what they were capable of doing to us because of how they viewed us. Once we were given our freedom and we did not take it (and by taking our freedom, I mean going home or at least separating our societies), knowing what we knew about them, can you really blame white people for anything that they did to us from that moment on? Can you really blame someone for taking advantage of a fool? There is a saying in Jamaica. It goes, "if you find a mule, ride it."

I was having a conversation with a Sudanese friend of mine once. We were talking about race relations in America and he was expressing his point of view on the subject, being a foreigner, or more specifically, an African black person. He said something to me that had a profound effect on the way that I viewed the subject from then on. What he said was that he didn't understand why African Americans got angry with white people for being racist. He said that African Americans act as if white people owe it to them not to be racist. That's just how they are. At first, I didn't agree, and chalked it up to him not fully understanding the African American experience. But the more I thought about it, the more I realized that he was absolutely right. White people do not owe it to us not to be racist. Nobody on Earth owes it to anyone else to view them a certain way. We owe it to ourselves as sentient, self-aware, self-respecting beings not to constantly place ourselves at the mercy of those who we know view us as inferior or expendable, or in any negative way whatsoever. What black people basically do and have been doing for centuries in this country is to run around after the white man begging him to accept us as his equals. No matter how long we pursue this course of action, and no matter how much progress we think we make pursuing this course of action, it will get us nowhere. The time and energy that we spend begging would be better spent proving that we are equal, and the way to do that requires us to completely change the way we function in the world as a people.

THE MACHINE CONSCIOUSNESS

The nature of the society that we live in is commercial and systematic. That societal commercial system that we live in is designed to maintain order primarily. We are also to assume that its purpose is to better our standard of living. These assumptions all exist in the light. The distinguishing characteristic of order is predictability. Order requires primarily that things, people and events are predictable. The problem with this, of course, is that life, and all the things, events and people in it, are not always predictable. This is where we encounter the dark.

Now that is not to say that there is not a certain degree, and admittedly, a high degree of order and predictability in life. Life itself is also systematic in nature. However, life also has a considerable degree of chaos or unpredictability built into it. And it is meant to be so. There has not yet been invented a technique or means of completely eliminating unpredictability from almost any system known to man, whether natural or man-made. That being said, serious problems can arise when that built in unpredictability of life is not acknowledged, accounted for and, most of all, respected, especially in human beings.

As I have been able to reason it, one of the main ways that life accounts for and accommodates chaos, which is a fundamental principle of the universe and as such, must be respected and accommodated, is through subtlety. When I say subtlety, I mean that there is not only one way to be anything in this life. There is not only one way to be a lion, there is not only one way to be the color red. Often, we hear this concept illustrated in moral terms in the saying "shades of grey." Individuality is also where this concept finds its home. My point, as it pertains to the application of this concept in this particular chapter is that, much like there is not only one way to be a lion, or only one shade of red, there is not only one way to be a human being, and a pretty decent one by all important standards at that.

Now, in all of this philosophical reasoning there is an end and the end point, as it pertains to this commercial societal system that we live in is that there is a method by which the intellects of the world control others in humanity who cannot yet think and reason on a level rivaling those intellects. You see, ultimately, a mental

DARK TRUTHS

Darwinian process is what decides who gets to control who in the ranks of humanity, and those who have attained a certain level of ability in thinking and reasoning, and who crave and desire power, do whatever they can to retard the development of higher level thought and reasoning in the rest of humanity in order to attain and maintain power and control over the masses.

I touched upon a key technique that those intellects use in the earlier chapter on fear. In this chapter I would like to detail another effective technique used by the elite, which is moral absolutism. I've dubbed this chapter "The Machine Consciousness" because this is the age of the Machine. Today, mechanical wonders abound and computers are all the rage. Even I myself am not writing this chapter by hand, but typing it on my very handy and convenient laptop. Society today runs like a colossal machine and in order for a machine to run properly, all components of the machine must operate "correctly."

In order to get erratic and unpredictable beings such as humans to operate "correctly," a program must be installed. This program is moral absolutism, or as I like to call it, the Machine Consciousness. Think about this: for those of you who have an advanced understanding of the fundamental mechanics by which computers operate, you know that because of the basic physics of how computers operate, computers think in a particular language. This language is binary. Because the individual electrons that constantly flow through a computer can only either pass through an open gate, or not pass through a closed gate, computers think entirely in 1s and 0s. This is binary language and all things that computers do, and all languages that one can use to program them, are built on the foundation of binary computer language.

So, this Machine Consciousness, as it is applied and used to program humans, is basically binary in nature, which is moral absolutism. Instead of 1 and 0, the terms used with humans in this programming are "right" and "wrong." Mental energy serves as electricity and a thing or idea is taught to humans to be determined as either "right" or "wrong," no in between. This is basically how machines think. This facilitates predictability in humans and makes them perfect cogs in a wheel; components of The Machine.

Of course, this thinking does not accurately reflect the reality that we live in, as there are many shades of gray, but it does facilitate order and predictability, which benefits people as whole, in some respects, but more so benefits those in control of the system. This allows them to direct the system to their ultimate aims more easily by cutting down on the element of chaos in the system, or at least chaos that they don't intend to be present for some particular aim, because even that, from their perspective, is order.

Now as I have maintained throughout this work, there is no value judgment on my end being placed upon any of the topics, ideas and issues presented here unless I specifically put forward such. This is simply a treatise

DARK TRUTHS

on the way things are. I think that the above system of control is decent in many respects and has its advantages in the pursuit of maintaining an orderly society. After all, some considerable level of order is desirable for the greater good of the whole in any society. Order benefits everyone in society and humans, by and large, prefer a great degree of order in their lives, especially when it comes to their core needs.

The place where we encounter the dark is when we begin to examine the ultimate aims of those in control of the system. At some point, it behooves those who are adherents to the dictates of the system to examine the aims of the elite and to ensure that the ultimate aims of those in power are actually in harmony with their own, at least to an acceptable degree. It is true that it is impossible to please all of the people all of the time, but it is also very detrimental to society, and the planet as a whole, when those in control of the system begin implementing plans and programs with selfish and self-serving aims and goals.

Consider the fact that there is an enormous wealth inequality persistent upon this planet. Also consider the rampant environmental damage being inflicted upon the planet. It is said that something to the effect of 95-99% of the wealth of this planet is owned by something like 1-5% of the population. An imbalance that extreme is very unlikely to have come about by chance. Something like this comes about by very intentional effort. Now, as I understand humans pretty well, I would say that there are few humans on this planet that would desire this economic state of affairs, at least of the portion of the population belonging to the disenfranchised majority.

I bring up the economic and environmental imbalance to illustrate that as thinking beings, we should be careful about accepting this Machine Consciousness because it appears to me that the elite of this world do not necessarily have the greater good of humanity in mind. There are many different walks and ways of life for a reason. Maintaining balance in an enormous and sprawling domain is not easily achieved by few. It takes many, with many different perspectives and ways of thought, all of which must be given due respect. The risk of an unhealthy degree of selfishness infecting the goals, aims and operation of the system increases exponentially when the elite are few and mostly of the same group. I say an unhealthy degree of selfishness because there is such a thing as a healthy degree of selfishness, but that is a subject for another work.

Thus far I have expounded much on the Machine Consciousness and how it is applied to humans, as well as the aim and effect of it, but only in broad and general strokes. I think it necessary before I move to the next chapter to detail its application and effect in a more individualized manner in order to add to and clarify the reader's understanding. One of the best and most poignant examples that I can think of is the concept of violence. We as citizens of pretty much any modernized, "civilized" nation, are taught that violence is never the answer and is always wrong. We are taught that if we want to effect change in the system, voting and non-violent protest are the only acceptable and effective ways to change the system. Non-violence is right. Violence is wrong. 1 or 0.

Since we would like to consider ourselves a free people, a fair and unbiased (i.e., free of the taint of the Machine Consciousness) examination of this premise requires us to define what freedom really is. I always like to look to nature to inform my thinking, because it is natural. That is to say there is no agenda in nature but that of The Creator, if you believe in such a thing, or Mother Nature, if you prefer that, and at the very least, one can say it is pure science. To lead the reader in the exploration of this premise, I will begin with canines. A domesticated dog behaves very differently than a wolf. A domesticated dog is not free. It enjoys many perks of being domesticated, but it is not free. A wolf is. We tend to call that "wild." The owner of a domesticated dog can kick his dog and the dog will not retaliate. It has been taught such behavior. In fact, an owner of a dog would not feel safe owning said dog were this not the case. Now, try that with a wolf.

The fact of the matter is, free (i.e., wild) beings do not hesitate to utilize violence to protect themselves and their interests. If you threaten a wolf in any way, or its cubs, you had better be ready for a fight. The same applies for free humans. The controllers of the system and programmers of the Machine Consciousness have convinced the "civilized" people of the world that violence is never ok. Meanwhile, the economy has become a routing system designed to funnel the world's wealth into the hands of the few while severely disenfranchising the many. In conjunction with this, the unchecked greed and lust for more power is damaging the planet so severely that future generations of the disenfranchised have much to fear. But not the controllers of the system. They enjoy a cozy position of smug superiority and security knowing that the people of the world are quite domesticated and would prefer to fight each other before they would dare challenge their owners, known and unknown.

Now, mankind has known warfare since the dawn of time. Almost every free people of the Earth, of any time period, have at one time or another had to fight to win or defend their freedom. Violently. This is not wrong. It is natural if one intends to remain free or become free. When the very fate of mankind is at stake, there is no better justification for violent revolt. At least, I know of none. But that is my own opinion. What is fact is that free people, like free animals, do not hesitate nor second guess utilizing violence or warfare to protect their lives, their freedom, and that which is important to them. That is an objective fact.

This Machine Consciousness operates in a variety of other ways and installs a host of other absolute value judgments in the minds of humans in order to keep them under control, and working toward accomplishing the aims of the elite, even if those very aims are detrimental to the adherents of the system themselves. I do not intend to detail all of the ways and value judgments and their operation in this chapter, as that is probably enough material for a separate book. Suffice it to say that, once you become privy to the fact that your mind has been compromised and programmed from youth with thoughts and concepts and ideas that do not serve you, a self-initiated cleansing process must ensue if one wishes to be free of the mal-programming. One must begin to question and examine one's core beliefs, things one may never have even considered questioning before. It's a confusing place to be in. The great philosophic minds of history were known to allow nature to guide their thought on subjects and inform them. If the reader wishes to initiate this daunting and intimidating process, my advice to you is to study nature. You will find much mental clarity and answers to many confusing issues right there in nature. In the meantime, I say to you this: beware the Machine Consciousness.

MONEY MATTERS (OR DOES IT?)

Money. In this day and age, it is the wellspring of the basic necessities of life and in many ways, wellbeing itself. Today not even the farmer, a master of the husbandry of natural resources and the basic necessities of life, is safe from the frantic need to create cashflow. Yea, not even the farm, the source of the very sustenance of our lives, is immune to the commercial press of the Machine. The very land that the farmer tends is owned, or mortgaged, or taxed by men of commerce, men of money.

In the light, we are to believe that money is simply a tool of commerce, a medium of trade. We are told that money is simply designed to make the valuation of items of commerce easier and more uniform, and that it simply facilitates trade. While all of these functions of money are truly executed, there is a dark side. In the former chapter, I mentioned that the economy of the world has become a routing system designed to more or less surreptitiously funnel the wealth of the world into the hands of the few. This is done through the means of the modern monetary system. This chapter is intended to be a somewhat simplified description of how it works.

In order to truly understand the modern monetary system, one must first understand what money actually is, and have at least a basic knowledge of the history of money over the millennia of man's existence. In truth I find it quite odd that people are so woefully ignorant on the subject of money considering that money is the prime deity of this day and age, despite what people may say to the contrary or however stringent their cultural practices may be. For those who may feel the burning need to argue the latter point, or to say that it doesn't apply to them personally, and that there is no god but whatever name they and their people may have for the concept of god, I say this: there is an etymology behind the word "worship," which I will spare the reader the explanation of at this time for the sake of brevity, that basically amounts to the fact that at its core, to worship something means to value something. What you worship is what you value. What you value is what you worship.

Man has used countless items as money throughout history. Mankind has used everything from shells, to beads, to livestock, to stones and gems as representations of wealth and stores of value over time. Precious metals such as gold and silver have come to be mankind's favorite medium for trade and representation of wealth, that is until fairly recently. This is not to say that gold and the like don't still hold a high place in the hearts of lovers of wealth, but in modern times paper money, and now digital money or "credit," has taken center stage in the world of commerce.

Precious metals became highly favored amongst men as money primarily because they are rare. They also are a fair representation of work. Because these metals had to not only be sought out, but pulled from the ground, they made a decent quid pro quo exchange when given in return for the labor of another or another's product upon which they labored. Work for work. These metals facilitated a stable monetary system because the natural limits of supply created an intrinsic value of the money that did not fluctuate much. The circumstances of the locality determined supply and thus were the prime determinants of the value of the metals, and that value could only really fluctuate at the rate of change of the circumstances of the locality.

It is where we encounter the difficulties with using precious metals for trade that the legend of The Great Paper Money Swindle begins. That legend, as I have heard it told, has its roots in Europe, but I suspect that it may have been happening elsewhere as well. The problem people encountered with using precious metal for trade is that metal is heavy and bulky and large amounts of it are difficult to transport across long distances. Add to that that highways were very dangerous places, rife with banditry (thus the common term "highway robbery"), and the prospect of conducting trade with neighboring cities that may produce items of value that may be rare in one's locality becomes a daunting proposition.

At this point in time, it was a common practice for people to store their money with metal workers, or blacksmiths, because they were known to have strong boxes or safes. People would bring their gold or silver coins to the blacksmith, count them out, and for a small fee, he would keep their money safe and give them a paper receipt that accounted for the amount of money he had stored for them. Soon enough, people discovered that it was much easier to keep account of trade balances using these paper receipts instead of actually withdrawing their metal coins and bullion and physically transporting and exchanging them for items.

Well, it was not long before the blacksmiths had a clever, yet sinister idea. You see blacksmiths, being skilled tradesmen in this time, were also men of means and were known to loan money from time to time. They noticed that people were no longer calling on their money reserves held by the blacksmiths, and the blacksmiths soon began to loan out more paper receipts than they had coins and bullion in total in their possession. Nobody bothered to ever withdraw their coin and bullion anymore because everyone was trading using the paper receipts they wrote out, so who would ever be the wiser? The blacksmiths would charge a small fee for the loan in addition to what was owed (interest), and the blacksmiths began increasing their wealth greatly using this swindle.

Today's monetary system is based on the ancient blacksmiths' swindle. The blacksmiths evolved into bankers, and because government and government official hands can always be found in the pot where the money is, the blacksmiths' paper receipts evolved into what is now called fiat currency. Fiat currency is a term that denotes money that has no intrinsic value, but is only utilized by people as money because the ruler(s) of a land decree it. Because people found paper money so convenient, and the blacksmiths/bankers were creating so much wealth with their scheme, of course the King/government wanted in, and fiat currency had its official birth.

Now, in the United States, our fiat currency of choice is called a Federal Reserve Note. What is the Federal Reserve? Well in the light, what we are told is that the Federal Reserve is the central bank of the United States. Its purpose is to tightly regulate the money supply and fiscal policy in order to keep our economy stable. One could argue that it's doing a terrible job, but a counter-argument could easily be raised that this is complex stuff that's being dealt with, and not an easy task to stabilize an entire economy. That could go double for an economy the size of that of the United States. So c'mon, you gotta give these guys a break, right?

DARK TRUTHS

Well, before you go giving the Federal Reserve an award for doing the best that it can with this incredibly complex financial system, there are probably a few things that you should know about the nature of the Federal Reserve. These facts are easily found, but yet and still exist in the dark and are not often or widely discussed. The first and most important fact is that the Federal Reserve is neither Federal, nor is it a Reserve. In fact, the Federal Reserve is a private banking cartel owned by ancient European banking families. The Federal Reserve is no more government owned than the company Federal Express is.

Now, for the thinking individual, this has some potentially dire implications. The Federal Reserve is the entity that actually owns, prints, and controls our money! That is an immense power to be surreptitiously divorced from that of the people and handed over to PRIVATE FOREIGN AGENTS! It could come across as somewhat treasonous on its face if you ask me. But then, that's if you ask me, and nobody did at this point.

<u>Now, throughout this work I have refrained from citing references, but I think that this particular subject matter is so very critical for the reader to not only understand, but to believe, that I will suggest to the reader a book that not only details the workings of our monetary system, but also details the surreptitious means by which the Federal Reserve was created and legislated into existence. The title of the book is called The Creature from Jekyll Island by G. Edward Griffin. This is a</u>

<u>well-known work, but only in circles of people who actually care enough about knowing the truth about such matters to seek it.</u>

So, The Great Paper Money Swindle continues to this day, based on the blacksmiths' original idea, and here I will give a simple description of how it works. The Federal Reserve, which is a for profit, privately owned banking business, owns and prints Federal Reserve Notes. There is no money in the United States considered legal tender for all debts, public and private, as stated on the Federal Reserve Notes themselves, lest it originates from the Federal Reserve, so even the digital money and credit that is issued to the public is accounted for as part of the money supply issued solely from the Federal Reserve.

The U.S. Treasury, which is by original law the entity rightfully entrusted with the responsibility of printing money and managing the money supply and fiscal policy of the nation, now instead issues or sells what are called Treasury Bills (T-Bills) and Treasury Bonds (T-Bonds) to the Federal Reserve which are for a specific amount plus interest. They are basically like any other corporate bonds which represent loan notes. In exchange, the Federal Reserve issues Federal Reserve Notes and credit totaling the amount of the T-Bonds and T-Bills issued, expecting the loan that they represent be repaid, plus interest. Please keep in mind that there is no other source of legitimate legal tender in existence in this country other than that issued by the Federal

Reserve. The Federal Reserve also uses a similar setup for issuing money and credit to its many offspring, the twelve Federal Reserve banks that issue currency to the many corporate banks that we are familiar with. This makes up the Federal Reserve banking system.

The Federal Reserve issues this currency to both the U.S. Treasury and the banking system at an interest rate that we have come to know as the Prime Rate. The various outlets of this currency issue it out at various inflated interest rates in order to make individual profits. This all sounds rather complex, but to simplify it all to where the laymen can easily see the crux of the matter, I ask you this: if I am the only source of a particular commodity in existence, and I tell you that I will loan you some of this thing, this commodity, but I expect that you will repay me in this same specific commodity, plus some more of this same specific thing that you can only get from me, how will you repay me without asking me for more of it? Or, put another way, where will you find more money to repay me with when I am the sole source of money? You will have to go further into debt with me to pay the original debt with me, won't you? Or, you will have to rob the proverbial Peter to pay me, Paul, won't you?

The way that this mechanism is used to control the money supply is simple. When the Federal Reserve wants to increase the money supply in the country, it buys more T-Bills and T-Bonds. But, when it wants to contract the money supply in the nation, it calls in its debts, or sells the Bonds and Bills of the Treasury and its underling banks. This mechanic gives them total control over the monetary system and the ability to cause bubbles and recessions at will. What is the point? When the money supply is expanded, money and credit flow freely, and people and the businesses they create buy more, hire more, create more and work more.... on credit. But when the Federal Reserve calls in its accounts receivable, the money supply suddenly contracts, and real property; real land, equipment, cars, houses, businesses, etc.; are swallowed up (i.e. repossessed, liened, or basically taken in some respect) by the banks, and ultimately, by the banking families of the Federal Reserve. It's basically a game of monetary musical chairs, conducted by the European banking families of the Federal Reserve Cartel.

This is the nature of the monetary system that we currently live under, and it is designed to have a built-in lack, a built-in deficit, a built-in and inescapable debt. This is why the government debt is always increasing, and this is why it will never be able to be extinguished. This is also the core reason why there never seems to be enough money in your own life, and why the average United States citizen is in perpetual debt. This is why virtually every country in the world is in perpetual debt: because this same banking cartel was able to institute a central banking system that works in this same fashion or worse in almost every country in the world.

Of course, the most obvious intention and effect of

this system is as I stated earlier: to funnel the wealth of the world into the hands of the few. I must make it clear to the reader that wealth has almost nothing to do with the ownership of money, least of all paper money or 1s and 0s in cyberspace. True wealth has to do with the ownership of resources, natural and otherwise. Also note that true wealth and power are very closely related, and it is here at this point that I will touch on my earlier assertion having to do with worship again.

It is this author's humble opinion, in fact I would say more than an opinion, but more like a conclusion based on much observation and analysis, that all of this amassing and hording of wealth by the elite few is about more than just luxurious living or even power. I mean, wealth for wealth's sake is fine and dandy on its face, but what on Earth would be the reasoning for hording more wealth than you or your children could ever spend in multiple lifetimes while watching so much of humanity struggle with the most basic of necessities all around you?

It is my belief that this extreme and grotesque hording of wealth is designed to have a mental and spiritual impact on mankind. For any reader who may be familiar with the principles of the Law of Attraction, this author is an adherent to that school of thought, but I also know how difficult it can be for most to think and manifest abundance when evidence all around them suggests lack is the reality. The spiritual effect of a belief in lack causes the most morally undesirable behavior in human beings. This is the purpose. Morally undesirable behavior in humans seems to justify oppression of humans to humanity. Oppression of humanity begets further morally undesirable behavior in humans and it is a self-perpetuating cycle. This cycle is the means by which those who are able to master and sustain this negative feedback loop stay in power in perpetuity.

Ultimately, the Law of Attraction is most definitely in full effect and is strikingly illustrated in the working of paper money if one looks below the surface. The Law of Attraction basically deals with the power of the human mind to create, not only things and ideas, but its circumstances. This power is activated when thought is propelled by faith. A piece of paper has little to no value alone. Paper money has little to no value alone. A Federal Reserve note has little to no value alone, no matter the denomination. What then is it that gives paper money power or value?

The answer may not be the first one that comes to the average mind. It is not the law, or government decree, or even the things people will give you in exchange for it. The answer is actually faith. At its core, people's faith in a dollar bill is what actually gives it worth, value, power. You accept paper money or digital credit in exchange for your time and toil daily because you have faith that someone will give you what you need and want in exchange for it, and the person who accepts your dollar bill in exchange for their goods or services does so because they have faith that the next will do the same, and so on. It is not the goods themselves that give the paper value, it is the faith of the owners of the goods that give it value because if at any time the owners of the resources/goods/services of the world lose faith in the dollar bill, its worth immediately plummets.

The stunning impact of the above revelation may escape most at first. However, once you actually realize and understand the above, that paper money operates completely on faith and it is YOUR FAITH in it that has given it such extraordinary and seemingly omnipotent power in this day and age over YOUR LIFE and almost every other, you will realize just how much my earlier statement about money being the prime deity of this age was not at all hyperbole, and applies to the great majority of humanity, even if they are woefully unaware of it. Printed quite clearly on the Federal Reserve note itself are the words "In God we trust." You see, in the light it sounds great to say that you worship some spiritual name and idea of God because you go to church on Sunday or the mosque or synagogue or whatever. In the dark however, what you worship is what you value, and what you value is what you worship.

CHAPTER

10

WE NOW RETURN TO YOUR REGULARLY SCHEDULED PROGRAMMING

———————————

Television programming. It is a simple term that most people think that they know the meaning of. In fact, there are many terms that people use every day and believe that they know the meaning of, but in truth, they are mistaken. Upon closer analysis, many every day terms reveal a deeper or contrary meaning to popular belief. Television programming is one of those terms.

The term "television programming" consists of two words. The word "television" refers to a device that we are all familiar with. The television is in almost every house in America and many houses around the world and is used to entertain and inform people. The word "programming" is the word that makes this term more interesting. The word "programming," as defined in the

Merriam-Webster Dictionary means "the planning, scheduling, or performing of a program." The word "program," as defined in the Oxford Dictionary has two meanings relevant to this chapter. The second definition given is "arrange according to a plan or schedule" but the first definition given in this dictionary is what draws my attention with regard to the term being discussed. The first definition given is "provide (a computer or other machine) with coded instructions for the automatic performance of a task."

Often, the term "television program" is used interchangeably with "television show;" thus, people take the term "television programming" to mean "the schedule and order of television shows to be played." This is as it is viewed in the light. I propose that the dark may conceal a slightly different and more sinister meaning. Most people believe that people program T.V.s. I believe that T.V. programs people and that is what is truly meant by the term "television programming."

Take advertisements, for example. Commercials are shown constantly during and in between T.V. shows. Certain product advertisements are run during certain shows that advertisers believe are watched by a demographic of people that would be interested in their product. One can see beer commercials during a football game, household product commercials during soap operas and daytime television in general, and toy commercials during cartoons.

The object of commercial advertising is two-fold.

First, advertisers may seek to have a commercial for their particular brand of a product seen enough times by individuals that when they need said product, and go to purchase said product, they will remember, and consequently purchase, the brand of said product advertised. Secondly, and more insidiously, advertisers may seek to convince people that they need something that they, in fact, do not. This aim of advertising is more insidious because to convince a person that they need something that they actually don't is to actually draw a person outside of their logical mind. It is, in essence, to literally induce a mild state of insanity in another human. This is done every day and because of that, the above description may strike the reader as a bit over-dramatic but it is nonetheless true. So, despite the commonplace nature of the offense, it is in the best interest of any thinking person who wishes to make sane decisions in their life at all times to recognize the insidious nature of the process above and to guard their mind against it.

T.V. shows are also used to program people; thus, the term "T.V. program." Firstly, they work hand-in-hand with commercials through the demographic they draw, as I stated above. Aside from that, most T.V. shows contain certain moral stories, social, political or even religious themes, and subtle commentary on what is and what is not acceptable behavior. News programs in particular are used to mold public opinion and create a favorable climate for war, drug policy, space travel, or any number of designs of the powers that be.

DARK TRUTHS

Another strong example of how television programs people can be seen in movies. Though movies do not start out on T.V., they often end up there after their run in the box office. I find that movies are most often used as a way to prepare people for near-future things, events, or technologies. For example, there was a movie that came out in 1998, just three years before the events of the 9-11 incident, called "The Siege," starring Denzel Washington. This movie depicted a terrorist attack in which Islamic extremists hijacked two New York City buses, rigged them with explosives and drove them, with hostages onboard, into the federal building in Manhattan and leveled it. Sounds familiar, doesn't it? Coincidentally (or maybe not so much so), the movie goes on from there to deal with the issues of torture and infringement on the rights of American citizens by the government in times of crisis. One may be tempted to think that this is mere coincidence, but I can give other, similar examples.

Some years ago, leading into the millennium and early in the millennium, I noticed at least two movies that came out depicting the President of the United States as a black man. These were the first movies in which I had ever seen such a depiction. One of the movies was named "Deep Impact," in which Morgan Freeman played the role of President of the United States. Lo and behold, by 2009 the United States was inaugurating Barack Obama the 44th President of the United States.

All of the above examples that I mentioned are crafty,

and some even obvious, techniques meant to influence human thought and behavior through entertainment. People may not want to admit it, but it is true. In the light, we are taught and would like to believe that the television is a benign device at our beck and call, whose sole purpose for existence is to entertain and inform us. In the dark however, television programming programs the people, as well as the television. Here is a thought for you to mull over. As a youth, I watched a lot of cartoons. As an adult, I came to the shocking realization that there may be more truth hidden amongst the fiction of those cartoons than I was aware of at the time, more truth than even adults suspect. The basic make-up of many cartoons began with a hero and a villain. The villain was always a megalomaniac with the perennial intention of world domination. One of the most common plots of this villainous character was to create a device capable of brainwashing the entire world population and turning all mankind into mindless slaves. The questions I pose to you are; what if people like this archetypal villain really exist? What if you were born into a world where this type of people already succeeded? How would you know? So, the next time you change the channel or program your cable or DVR, you might wanna ask yourself; who's really programming who?

Heru the First Son is the nom de plume of Jason Thomas. Born in Queens, NY and raised primarily in Brooklyn, Heru has experienced many of the trials and tribulations that have become all too common for black men in America, including the struggles of being involved in the streets, being incarcerated on Riker's Island, and doing time in federal prison for marijuana and gun possession. Through it all, Heru has maintained a thoughtful and conscious disposition, and approaches his writing in a philosophical manner that rises above his circumstances, sharing lessons learned from his experiences and fresh perspectives on many topics especially relevant today. Heru also has a Hip Hop single out on all major music streaming platforms entitled "Welcome to the Machine" that shares all of the powerful insight and relevance of his writing. He currently resides in Raleigh, NC.

www.ingramcontent.com/pod-product-compliance
Lightning Source LLC
Chambersburg PA
CBHW020302030426
42336CB00010B/875